HOW TO BE A
BAD
GIRL
IN BED

THIS IS A CARLTON BOOK

Design and text copyright © Carlton Books Limited 2011

This edition published in 2013
by Carlton Books Limited
20 Mortimer Street
London W1T 3JW

10 9 8 7 6 5

A CIP catalogue record for this book is available from the British Library.
ISBN 978 1 84732 412 2

Printed and bound in Italy

Senior Executive Editor: Lisa Dyer
Managing Art Director: Lucy Coley
Designer: Gülen Shevki-Taylor
Copy Editor: Jane Donovan

HOW TO BE A
BAD
GIRL
IN BED

LISA SWEET

CARLTON
BOOKS

CONTENTS

Introduction

Every woman, no matter how sugar, spice and everything nice she is, has the occasional urge to be bad. And why not? Bad girls are wild and spontaneous. Bad girls don't follow the rules. Bad girls are still good to go at 3 am. Bad girls are fun. And, of course, bad girls are amazingly good in bed. They love getting it on, have zero inhibitions and sex drives that work overtime. And they know what they crave in bed and how to get it. Oh-oh-oh yeah! As they say, good girls go to heaven and bad girls go everywhere!

Just remember there's a huge difference between being bad and being downright nasty. As a rule of thumb, bad girls take him along for the adrenalin ride; nasty girls leave him on the side of the road feeling trampled and tossed out like yesterday's trash.

Fact is, bad girls are the reason why many men shy away from women who seem too nice. Nice is fine for meeting the parents but it can be too clingy and dependent in a relationship; also too passive and by-the-book in bed. Face it – good girls don't surprise their lovers at work and ravage them on their desk. His inner bad boy wants a companion – a woman who knows what she wants carnally and isn't embarrassed or uncomfortable about getting it. These are the qualities that make his penis curl.

Luckily, bad girls are not born that way. Even the sweetest angel can channel her devilish side. We're not talking about stocking up on whips and chains (though if that's your fancy, go for it). It's about not being afraid to go after what you want, daring to try new things and indulging in your passions. And it doesn't matter if you're single or happily in a relationship, there's still plenty you can do to wickedly take charge of your orgasms, your libido, your passion and your sex life. Read on for quick and easy ways to get very, *very* naughty...all the tips are coded "Vanilla", "Naughty" or "Baaaadd" so you can start a little saucy and shimmy your way up to hardcore bad or skip straight ahead to the really, *really* raunchy.

Four Excuses for Good Girls to Be Bad

...and they're all good for your health!

Scientists have already given the thumbs up to being addicted to chocolate (it's high in antioxidants) and raising a glass of red vino (heart-healthy). Now they're finding a silver lining to other so-called bad girl behaviours.

1 **Bad girls are okay with getting pissed off.** Turns out raging – as opposed to its 'nice girl' stepsister's "anxiety" and "fear" – prompts the brain to release less cortisol, the powerful stress hormone linked to problems such as obesity, bone loss and heart disease.

Bad girls require regular java jolts. While the caffeine kick certainly boosts bad-girl energy, the real health benefits are the anti-inflammatory compounds coffee is chock-full of, which may minimize risk of Parkinson's disease, cancer and Type 2 diabetes. **2**

3 **Bad girls never clean up after themselves.** However being a slob may help them breathe more easily and stay healthier. Not only is it harder for allergens to breed in a messy area, you need a little dirt to boost your immunity.

Bad girls like beer. But that pint could be an even better heart-disease fighter **4** than red wine. It packs the same heart-protecting antioxidants as red wine, is high in vitamin B6, which reduces coronary risk, and is rich in silica, which strengthens bones. Bottoms up!

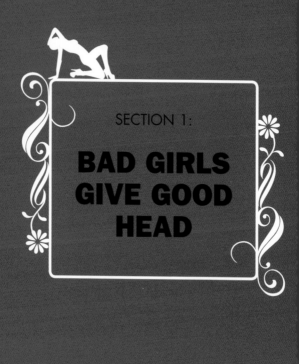

SECTION 1:

BAD GIRLS GIVE GOOD HEAD

Get your mind out of the gutter! Not that kind of head – this is about having mental moxie. Nothing is sexier in a woman than an "I'm-so-that" attitude. Unfortunately, the whole business of connecting romantically with the opposite sex seems to be purpose-built to crush confidence. But bad girls don't waste time watching the ice melt when a crush is nearby or worrying if their breasts are too small/their bum is too big/their nipples are too pointy or if they're ever going to come: they take risks, they act flirty and they don't wait, hope, and pray that things will go their way.

Luckily, it doesn't take years of self-work to get that kind of mojo. Confidence is a self-fulfilling prophecy. If you have belief in yourself, who's to argue? On the pages that follow you'll find the seven sinful Cs for mastering a cocksure state of mind.

Have Courage

Overcome the urge to sit back on the sidelines. So what if that hottie at the bar is a Calvin Klein model lookalike? Don't think anyone is out of your league. The point is not to worry about saying or doing the wrong thing. What's a wrong thing? And who said so? Do you care?

Your Bad Girl's Cheat Sheet for Being Bold.

❀ When you encounter a potential hook-up, make deep eye contact. Look him straight in the eye and hold it, hold it – until he wouldn't dream of looking anywhere else unless you told him to. *Vanilla*

❀ Appreciate the competition. Telling a man you think another woman has a great body or sexy moves packs a two-fold punch – first, it shows that you're so in tune with your own appeal, you don't freak over calling his attention to other women. Second, it makes him immediately picture girl-on-girl sex. *Naughty*

✳ Dally with his team. Getting flirty with his friends lets him know you can hold your own and triggers his territorial instincts. Of course, if, in the course of playing around, you happen to realize you prefer his best mate, go for it. Bad girls don't worry about the rules. *Baaaadd*

✳ Don't wait for him to pony up a compliment. Give them – to yourself. Know that you look beautiful and are sexy... and then make sure he knows it, too. If you're not ready to say, "Don't I look finger-lickin' good tonight?", you can convey the same message without uttering a word. A few examples: cross and uncross your legs, brush a fingertip across your lips, smize (that's runway-speak for smile with your eyes). And never underestimate the power of sticking your neck out. Whether or not you have fabulous curves elsewhere, you have something else that all men drool over: a smooth, oh-so-feminine (read: no Adam's apple) neck. So use it: Lift your locks, slide a finger along your collarbone, play with your necklace, ask him to refasten your choker, whatever it takes to focus his eyes where you want. *Vanilla*

❋ Be able to take a compliment. If a guy says, "God, you have an awesome [body part]!," a bad girl smiles and shakes said body part – she doesn't deny or giggle and cover it up. *Vanilla*

❋ Keep a sandwich by the bed. Bad girls aren't afraid to show that they get hungry. A passion for food means passion, period. Nothing's more of a turn-off to a guy than a salad-no-dressing kind of girl. Don't be shy about getting into a little food foreplay, either – lick your lips, suck the sauce off your fingers, sword-swallow an asparagus stalk. If that's too much of a feeding frenzy, simply lean over and nab some food off from his plate or feed him some choice titbits from yours. *Vanilla*

✸ Act French. Les femmes fatales of France are anything but shy. Seduction is as basic a part of life as breathing. They don't sit around plucking the petals from flowers, wondering, "He loves me, he love me not". They'll discard his bouquet of daisies and demand fine wine, fine food and fine treatment. They aren't afraid to have affairs, smell like sex, skip the hair wax, wear stilettos in daylight hours, frilly lingerie to bed and red lipstick all of the time. Femmes fatales are completely feminine and totally kick-ass at the same time. *Naughty*

✸ Don't hang around making goo-goo eyes, hoping he'll come to you. When you see what you want, go for it before the moment slips by. There are lots of ways to go about this: you could just go up, say hi and ask his name or his number. But if the easy approach seems way too hard, on the pages that follow are some bad-girl moves to get you instantly connected in any location (don't think of these as games; rather, they're ice-breakers).

- **Anywhere:** If you have a built-in camera, ask him to take a snap of you and your friends/a street sign/a nearby cool car or anything else in the vicinity. Then ask if you can take his picture and offer to send it to him – now you have a way to contact him. *Vanilla*

- **At a club:** Grab his hand and start dancing. *Naughty*

- **On the street:** Ask him for directions – and then follow up with questions about where's good to go in the neighbourhood. *Vanilla*

- **At a pub:** Order two drinks and take one over to him. If this is too straightforward, you can pretend the bartender accidentally made more than you ordered. *Naughty*

- **At the gym:** Ask him to spot you. *Vanilla*

- **At the beach:** Ask if he has sunscreen and if he can rub some on you. *Baaaadd*

Be Clever

Bimbos are not interesting. Brains are an essential part of the bad-girl package. This doesn't mean knowing the square root of pi; it's knowing how to tell a great story or a dirty joke (see Get Chatty pages 28–30 for some samples), talking about things you're passionate about, taking an interest in the world around you and being curious to try new things. Showing your smart side means going beyond those initial ho-hum "What do you do?" questions and going a bit deeper – Why did you pick that career? Choose this place to live? Like that song? These are the conversation starters that make bad girls stand out. *Vanilla*

3 Be Casual

Bad girls don't confuse a good time or great sex with love. It's not that they don't want the happily-ever-after ending, but they know that a relationship is just one part of life. They feel whole on their own and don't need a partner to be complete. This laid-back attitude means they go with the flow...

In the bedroom:
Bad girls act on desire, not what-if's. They know that sex is sex and not a statement about the relationship. Not that they're casual about their pleasure – they just realize that having an orgasm with a man doesn't mean you're destined for a grand romance. *Naughty*

If he throws his socks on the floor: That's because they're too busy ripping the rest of his clothes off. *Naughty*

When they have a lover's quarrel: Bad girls know that however bad the argument, the make-up sex will be great (because they'll initiate it). *Baaaadd*

During a break-up:
Bad girls don't moon over
the good times, call their ex and
hang up, stalk his place of work, or the
thousand and one other things good girls do
to torture themselves when a relationship ends.
Because they know there are plenty of potential
The One's out there, they remind themselves of
every fault he had, from selfishly scoffing the
last crisp in the package to being perennially
late. They donate anything he left in their
flat to Oxfam and make a booty call to
a friend with benefits (every bad girl
has at least one of these tucked
away). *Baaaadd*

When he doesn't call: If a bad girl is in the mood, they may call him. But she might also call someone else. What she doesn't do is think that him not calling means she is ugly, undesirable or unsexy. She knows her worth and doesn't lay all her bets on one single guy. Which is why, if he does call, she isn't necessarily hang-up-the-phone available. This isn't about playing hard to get – it's about playing hard. Simply put, she has a life of her own. *Baaaadd*

When he's just not into them: Bad girls don't waste their time messing with a guy who holds back. Life is just too damned short. *Naughty*

4 Get Carnal

Not down and dirty in the bedroom (that comes later). Carnal means being comfortable with being sensual – bad girls don't worry if they're the slinkiest she-devil in the room. Being a bombshell is a state of mind – here's how to get a bad attitude.

Develop a signature style to captivate and charm. Once you own your own body, you own the room. It might be moving very slowly, swinging your hips, giving good posture by holding your head high, your neck long and your chest out, or simply rolling your eyes – whatever it is, it's all yours. *Vanilla*

Check him out. Good girls let guys take the lead. Bad girls size a guy up from head to just below the waist, letting him know they mmm-mmm appreciate what he has on offer. *Naughty*

Show you want him.
Lean your back against
him, then subtly grind
your bottom into his
front acreage. *Baaaadd*

Let your inner
sex kitten out.
You want it,
you like it
and you enjoy
it, so why hide it?
Touch, kiss and caress
to your libido's delight.
And when you say
good night, leave him
happy and horny with
a chaste kiss on the
lips and a squeeze
of his family jewels.
Baaaadd

Be Crazy

This doesn't mean sending "I miss you" texts five minutes after meeting him or being jealous of his relationship with his dog. Bad girls are crazy in that they take risks. They constantly try one new – hopefully outrageous – thing. And they don't settle in a rut – they do what's unconventional or unexpected. They might be Cartier and caviar one night, then hit reverse and throw on some jeans and toss back a few nachos grandes the next. That versatility shows a woman who is comfy in her own skin and makes him feel excited about who he's with tonight – librarian or pole dancer? *Vanilla*

Six Bad-Girl Dates to Go On Tonight

1
Rent a vespa. Bad Girl Move: Go full throttle so he has to hold on for dear life. *Naughty*

2
Take a boxing class. Bad Girl Move: Go ahead and hit him with everything you've got. *Baaaadd*

3
Play laser tag. Bad Girl Move: Take advantage of those in-the-dark opportunities for some below-the-belt gropes. *Baaaadd*

4
Try go-kart racing: Bad Girl Move: Cut him off at the pass. *Naughty*

5
Shoot pool. Bad Girl Move: Check out his angles. *Vanilla*

6
Go to the races. Bad Girl Move: Don't bet money – instead, the winner gets to choose what happens in bed later. *Baaaadd*

Be Cryptic

Being bad isn't just about what you say and do, it's also what you leave out. Divulging your life story is not how you create a connection. There is such a thing as too much information too soon. Bad girls create a sense of the unknown by building anticipation – out of bed as well as in. They move two steps forward and one back, then escalate things with a bit more before backing off again. So if he asks what happened in your last relationship, you don't moan on about how he ran off with your roommate. You simply say, "Dumped him – want to get some fries?" Basically, it's better to be brief and a touch mysterious than to read like an open book with nothing interesting left to discover. *Vanilla*

Get Chatty

Bad girls know how to use their mouth. Not there. Rather, they know how to hold their own in a conversation. Here's how to get the ball rolling.

Keep It Clean

Surprisingly, bad girls do not curse. They know if they swear like a bloody sailor all day, there's not going to be much allure to their dirty talk in bed later. *Vanilla*

Argue

Bad girls are not afraid to voice their opinion, even if it contradicts his. They might have a different sports team or vote a different colour. They know they can work out that built-up friction mano-a-mano on the mattress. *Vanilla*

Dole Out the Compliments

Bad girls know that a good stroke – of his ego, that is – is the quickest way to make a guy pant. So go ahead and give props to his sense of style, his choice of music or his skill at Black Ops. *Naughty*

Don't Go Over-the-Top

Combine the build-up above with a subtle knock down to keep him on the edge of his seat – "I really loved that look... last year/My little sister loves that band/You almost beat my score... " *Baaaadd*

Say Something Outrageous Without Batting an Eyelid

"That's a nice suit. It would look great on my bedroom floor." His jaw may drop but he'll love it. *Baaaadd*

Don't Waste Your Time

Introduce yourself with, "So are you in love with anyone right now?" *Naughty*

(If he is, this doesn't mean you have to back off with your attentions – you just know what's what.) *Baaaadd*

Master Double Entendres

Mix suggestive words with dual meanings into normal conversation. Ask him for a backrub because your neck is *stiff*. Or have him help you fill in a crossword puzzle that's too *hard*. Tell him you'll be late at work because you're *tied up*. Complain that the weather makes you *so hot*. Talk about the *amazing positions* you did in yoga.
Naughty

Appreciate a Good Dirty Joke

And even better, tell one that's 10 times dirtier. Here are three ways to tickle his bone:

Q: How does a woman scare a gynaecologist?
A: By becoming a ventriloquist!

Q: What did the banana say to the vibrator?
A: Why are YOU shaking? She's going to eat me!

Q: What's long, hard and full of seamen?
A: A submarine.
Baaaadd

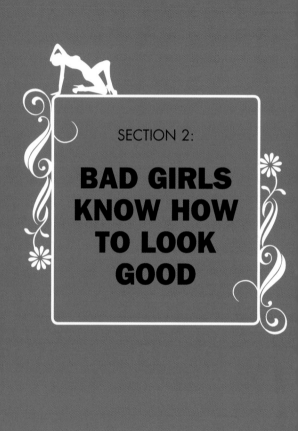

SECTION 2:

BAD GIRLS KNOW HOW TO LOOK GOOD

Bad girls get off on being the centre of male attention. They may capture it with a plunging neckline, a bare midriff, fishnets, high heels, skirts hemmed at mid-thigh, a strapless anything, or a lacy thong (if she wears any underwear at all). Or they might get the same result by wearing his old flannel shirt or a pair of jeans and a simple cotton T-shirt.

That's because bad girls know that sexy isn't about being the hottest, slimmest, tallest, bustiest and/ or best dressed in the room. It's about knowing how to walk the walk and strut her stuff, whatever she has on – whether it's a neckline down to there or his favourite sweater. Just a peek of a shoulder exposed in a side-cut shirt can be fabulously glamorous when it's worn with attitude.

Here's your head-to-toe plan for putting together the right bad-girl package for you – and also, how to unwrap it for him... slowly.

Getting Dressed

Peek inside a wild woman's closet and you'll find: slinky, barely-there panties and G-strings; a couple of garter belts; thigh-high, seamed and fishnet stockings in every hue; cotton briefs; bras that push up, unhook at the front, back and on the sides; nipple tassels; a few leather belts; shirts with every level of neckline; and skirts that range from way up here to way down there; outfits in every kind of material from leather and see-through lace to flannel; plus shoes that totter from 5 inches high to playful plimsolls.

And the point? Bad girls do *not* – repeat *do not* – slip into a piece of Lycra the size of an iPod each and every day. They have lots of different gear to express their every sexual mood. But you don't have to (re)vamp your threads (unless you want to). Sometimes, all it takes are a few minute adjustments to your daily wear to transform yourself into a vixen. Just mix and match a few of these tips – and be prepared to spend more time out of your clothes than in them.

Lose the Ratty Underwear

Your mom was right: You should always have nice underwear on. She was thinking in case of an accident, but bad girls know that slipping a silky something over your derrière and frontièrre and everything in between makes you feel oh-so-down-and-dirty good. If you don't have a G-string handy, at least put on something other than those dingy briefs with the frayed elastic. You want underthings that will make you more, not less, likely to indulge your bad girl and go for it when you run into a smokin' specimen.

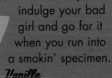

Vanilla

At Work

Obviously, you want to look like a professional, not like a pro, but you can still dress like a provocateur without looking as if your boss is a pimp:

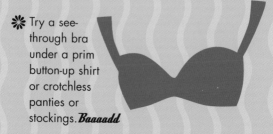

❋ Try a see-through bra under a prim button-up shirt or crotchless panties or stockings. *Baaaadd*

❋ Play with colour. Anything in hot sassy red is bolder than a little black number and will give you a slow burn all day. *Naughty*

❋ Put on touchy-feely clothes. Silk, suede, cashmere, even faux fur and fleece all feel amazing against your skin and have a pet-me allure that practically begs strangers to caress you. *Vanilla*

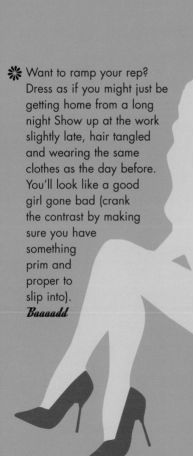

✳ Want to ramp your rep?
Dress as if you might just be
getting home from a long
night Show up at the work
slightly late, hair tangled
and wearing the same
clothes as the day before.
You'll look like a good
girl gone bad (crank
the contrast by making
sure you have
something
prim and
proper to
slip into).
Baaaadd

Out On the Prowl

Dress strategically. This means whatever makes you feel glam. The way you feel when you leave your house is going to set the tone for the rest of your day/night/morning after the night before so don't sacrifice comfort. If you love micro-minis with thigh-high boots and feel great wearing them, then go for it. But if that look means you'll spend the next five hours tugging at your hemline and sucking in your belly, then it's not such a good idea. Yes, less is more – in the case of make-up, hairspray, jewellery and facial hair. But when it comes to clothes, baring all isn't necessarily the sexiest option. Bad girls know that men are more interested in wondering what's underneath – think of it as the "librarian with glasses and hair in a bun" syndrome. So, no need to strip down to your skivvies or swank around in thigh-high boots to get your outfit noticed. Here are some *Vanilla* options that are just as bad-girl sexy as a body-hugging catsuit:

❈ A long skirt with a high slit will have him playing peekaboo with your legs

❈ A sheer top over a bra is so much sexier than a reveal-all low neckline

❈ A tight turtleneck shows off your silhouette

❈ A loose shirt with a few buttons strategically undone

❈ A strappy tank top (bra optional) seems bad-girl fun and casual

❈ His white work shirt (trust us – it seems like you're marking your territory)

❈ Anything in an animal print brings out your wild side while metallic tints make you sparkle

❈ A classic Oxford white and jeans combo oozes natural sex appeal.

39

On a Date

❋ Dress for ease – of removal, that is. But also dress appropriately. The most titillating temptress knows what makes an outfit suggestive is not so much what she wears, but how she wears it. *Naughty*

❋ Dress as sexy as you want – not as sexy as you think *he* wants to see you. Bad girls wear accoutrements like push-up bras and low-slung trousers for their own satisfaction, not his.

✳ Dress comfortably. A bad girl doesn't slob out but she doesn't wear clothes that make her feel less than all-that either.

✳ Dress smart. Bad girls look at the weather report before heading out and don't end up freezing in a mini and sleeveless in a blizzard because they wanted to show some skin.

✳ Dress for the occasion. Bad girls know that wearing a clingy dress and stilettos for a walk in the park isn't seductive; it's embarrassing.

✳ Dress your size. Tight clothes may hug your bodacious curves, but X-rated seductresses know that it's anything but alluring to a guy when you have to ask him to crowbar off your jeans.

Six Unexpected Bad-Girl Looks

1 Forget cleavage – show some bare skin with a backless top or dress or expose your neck and shoulders with a halter or strapless number. *Naughty*

2 Cover up bare flesh with a well-cut dress that hugs your curves in all the right places. *Naughty*

3 Skip the twilight vamp and opt for a morning-fresh suggestive girly look with a pink button-down shirt tied at the navel and white jeans. *Vanilla*

4

Go for thin instead of sheer material that just hints at your skimpy underthings. *Naughty*

5

A little lace goes a long way in amping up your *ooh-la-la* factor. *Vanilla*

6

Wear a close-fitting nude hued dress to make him look twice. *Naughty*

Spice Up Your Love Life

Sometimes all it takes to sling off your good girl and slip into a bad-girl attitude is wearing something completely out of the norm. Try these styles on for size to feel like a reckless adventuress leading a wildly exciting private life.

❋ What's your naughty fantasy? French maid? Schoolgirl? School teacher? Dress the part – and then be sure to act it out. *Baaaadd*

❋ Challenge him to dress you. *Naughty*

❋ Actually put on that thong/bustier/corset he bought you. Wear it to his parents. *Naughty*

❋ Ditch the sweat pants. Leggings are just as comfy and 10 times sexier. *Vanilla*

✳ Go take your panties
off in the bathroom –
but don't stop
there. Put
them in his
pocket,
invite him
to play footsy
between your
legs or drop your napkin
and ask him to pick it up,
making sure he gets a good
view when he leans over.

Baaaadd

Getting Undressed

Sure, sexy clothes are, well, sexy. But a sexier sight? You – naked to the core. After all, the real reason why you are getting devilishly dolled up is so you end up in your birthday suits, skin-to-skin. Here's how to get undressed with bad-babe style.

❋ Sensual sex, sultry seductress-style, is possible only if you can first appreciate and enjoy your own body. What this means is lightening up on the self-criticism. Bad girls love their bodies, kinks and all. Do whatever it takes to feel your sexiest, be it a pedicure, getting waxed, lathering up in lotion every day or having a weekly massage. *Vanilla*

❋ Vow to spend a minimum of 15 minutes a day in the buff (that's probably 10 minutes more than you already do). *Naughty*

Get almost naked – wear nothing else but…

- One of his work shirts *Vanilla*
- Stockings *Naughty*
- Boots or high heels… or both! (see Flirty Feet, pages 54–5 for ideas) *Baaaadd*
- A long coat and knee-high boots *Baaaadd*
- A long strand of pearls *Baaaadd*
- Nipple tassles *Baaaadd*
- A chain-link belt around the waist *Naughty*
- Ears and tail à la Playboy bunny *Baaaadd*
- A come-hither smile *Vanilla*

❋ Flaunt your so-fab stuff with a private strip show. Leave the lights on and choose a va-voom tune to take each item of clothing off, slowly, one by one. Crank up the carnal temperature with a squirming lap dance. *Baaaadd*

Get a Bad Girl Makeover

Simple style tricks that will bring out your inner coquette and make you feel like doing something very, *very* bad tonight.

Hair Down There

Don't just trim back the edges – remove the entire lawn with a Brazilian wax. There's something breathtakingly naughty about leaving yourself exposed down there. Does it hurt? Oh yeah – but you're bad, so you can take it.

Baaaadd

Get a mound to die for – some salons will dye your pubic hair to match your (crotchless, natch) undies. Or go for tarty tints such as hot pink, lime green or royal blue. *Baaaadd*

Wax yourself a sex symbol. Instead of the usual landing strip, groom your muff into a sexy heart shape or butterfly. *Baaaadd*

Make It Up

So long, prim and pretty. Summon your wickedly cool alter ego with heavily lined dark eyes that amp up your glower power and raw sexuality. *Naughty*

Slightly smudged black eyeliner = smouldering sexpot whose been out all night. *Baaaadd*

Create a
dramatic kiss-off pout
that stays put by layering lips
with blood-red pencil, lipstick and
gloss. Make sure you reapply just the
gloss in front of him. *Naughty*

Sexessorize

Slap on a temporary tattoo. *Vanilla*

Make it permanent. *Naughty*

Make him get one too. *Baaaadd*

Skip your usual rocks for a candy necklace – only offer a nibble to guys who share your wicked sweet tooth. Or get a candy bra for some late-night snacking. *Baaaadd*

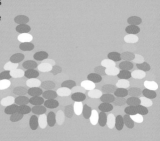

Diamonds may be forever, but bad girls know the cheekiest bangle to wear in bed is a vibrating tongue or clit ring. *Baaaadd*

Bad girls are never on a diet so they don't mind indulging in edible bras or panties (there is even a chocolate brassiere available). *Naughty*

Glam up your hands...
Manicures (red or metallics only) turn everyday mitts into instruments of mass seduction. Suddenly, every gesture you make seems mesmerizing; every object, person or (ahem) body part you touch gets stroked in a more sensual way.

Flirty Feet

Shoes are a bad girl's most important accessory. Here's a rundown on how to pair up your feet.

Stilettos:
A 2008 study by an Italian doctor found that wearing heels directly works the pleasure muscles linked to orgasm. So much sexier than Kegels. *Naughty*

Open-Toe Pumps:
Best worn with jeans for a laid-back, ready-for-anything message.
Baaaadd

Sequinned:
You don't need to go to a party in these shoes: you *are* the party.
Naughty

Gladiator or Strappy Sandals:
Bring it on, bondage girl!
Naughty

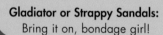

Platforms:
You can't be too rich or too thin. Or too tall... These skyscrapers put you head-and-shoulders over the competition. Go ahead and sashay! *Baaaadd*

FM Heels:
Says it all. *Baaaadd*

Thigh-high Boots:
Mad, bad and dangerous to know. *Baaaadd*

Leather Boots:
Ride 'em, cowgirl! *Naughty*

Black Flats:
You may be bad, but you have a stylish sense of comfort. *Vanilla*

Trainers:
Kick-ass! *Vanilla*

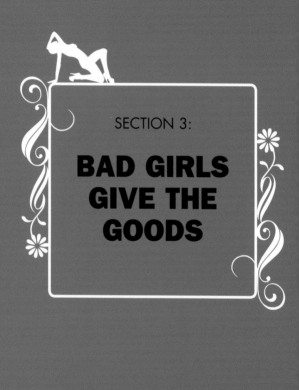

SECTION 3:

BAD GIRLS GIVE THE GOODS

Newsflash: Bad girls are not a bunch of panting leather-clad nymphos scrounging for their next hump-mate. Rather they (perhaps you?) are voracious connoisseurs when it comes to pleasure, forever searching for new experiences. Their sex life is never dull because they never lose the urge to explore. Even if they're happily hooked up, they'll spice things up with occasional forays like a backseat blowjob or a new, twisted position

It is this spirit of adventure that men go ga-ga over: This is what it means to be good in bed (well, this *and* swallowing). And it's why even the baddest dude will kneel, drool and pay homage to a bed devil because he knows that life – and sex – with her will never become boring.

Luckily any woman can get it on like a vampy vixen. All it takes is un-doing your old attitudes about sex and daring to say yes, yes, *yes* to these unabashedly risqué tips and tricks to being oh, so very bad.

Bad Girl Dare 1: Un-hinge Your Mind

Bad girls are flexible. Yes, their bodies can probably bend in 100 different ways, but it's their minds that count here.

The Tip: Sex doesn't have to be on Saturday night only. Thursday morning might be nice for a change. The missionary position may still satisfy (especially when you pull out a few of the tricks that follow), but with over 60 moves in the Kama Sutra alone (and that's only the basic ones), why limit yourself to just one?

The Trick: Everyone has their favourite sex move – the fallback that they know they're good at and always produces the goods. Take what you know and embellish it. If it's your oral skills, use your tongue in an unexpected way – side to side instead of up and down. Maybe it's kissing. If so, alternate your usual mouth moves with nibbles and sucks. If it's the old in-and-out, squeeze hard on the "in" and release on the "out". If you can't think of anything, just do the opposite of what you would usually do – hard for soft, wet for dry, and so on. *Naughty*

Twist It Up

In a bad girl's book, there's no such thing as a boring position. Try some of these nervy moves for shaking up your in and out.

**Bad Girl
Move for Standing
Up Positions:**
If you're going to put the effort in to stay on your toes, at least give it a scandalous note by moving the action to a public space such as a restroom or lift. *Naughty*: Lifting one leg high and tucking it around his limb makes it easier to stay vertically connected.

Bad Girl Move for Girl On Top:
Lean way, way back. Not only will this lengthen your curves and give him a full frontal view, either of you can work your happy button. *Naughty*: Arch your back to nudge his penis against your G-spot.

Bad Girl Move for Missionary:
Lifting your knees to your chest and hooking your ankles over his shoulder will make for some ultra-deep penetration that you'll feel along the back walls of your vagina. *Naughty*: Slip a vibrator over your clitoris – the extra buzz will also put a bounce in his bling.

Bad Girl Move for Rear Entry:
Have him tilt slightly back so you can be more in control of the action. *Naughty*: Swivel your hips so his pointer gives your vagina a full-body massage.

Bad Girl Dare 2: Do the Unexpected

Surprise and suspense are the ultimate tempters. When he's not sure what to expect, he'll be panting for more.

The Tip: Most couples usually fall into a rut of sex in the same place and in the same way every time. Ambushing him with a change in venue keeps you both on the edge.

The Trick: Challenge yourself to a week of out-of-bed love. Here's how to get down and dirty just about anywhere, anytime:

❋ **In a restaurant:** Perfect the art of the under-the-table handjob. Cover him with a napkin (to mop up spills) and squeeze and tug, using more pressure than usual because of the extra friction. *Baaaadd*

❋ **In the kitchen:** Crank up the heat by cooking in the buff. Turn your bodies into the dinner plate. *Baaaadd*

❋ **In the shower:** Lower the shower head and you'll make your own lather (man optional). *Baaaadd*

❋ **At work:** If you can't manage an on-site rendezvous, dial his digits and give him some dirty dictation. *Naughty*

❋ **When you're out with friends or family:** Work some of these racy remarks into the conversation –

- "My fingers are dripping with this yummy sauce."
- "Can I taste your pork and beans?"
- "Want a lick of mine?"

❋ He'll be burning with desire by the time you get into the car. *Naughty*

Bad Girl Dare 3: Be Unrepetitive

Bad girls don't repeat themselves. They know that no matter how wild and crazy a move is, if you do it over and over, it loses its thrill.

The Tip: The key is to work outside of your comfort zone just enough so that you can enjoy yourself but not so much that it's all about figuring out what comes next rather than being in the moment. Bad girls earn their good-in-bed rep because they're not just willing to experiment – they're also willing to fail (there's no such thing as one-orgasm-fits-all when it comes to sexperimenting) and they know not to overdo it.

The Trick: Invest in a sex-tip calendar and then use it – daily. (*Vanilla*, *Naughty* and *Baaaadd* – depending on that particular date's suggestion).

Bad Girls Change their Lover Every Night of the Week

These bad babes know how to sleep around without cheating on your partner. Role playing gives you an endless scenario of who/what/when/where and how to fool around (you know why – because it feels *soooo* good). Pretending you're S&M players and letting him have his wicked way is a two-for-one in that you get to live out every girl's wet dream of being overpowered in a take-me-now fantasy while he enjoys his bad-boy fantasy of playing rough and randy. Other spunky flights of fancy to try on a bad-girl attitude without risk: play at being strangers at a bar, foreign exchange students (he's a virgin), the classic horny handyman and housewife or whatever combo yanks your chain in a sweet way.

Naughty

Bad Girl Dare 4: Unclench, Already

Bad girls aren't necessarily going to go for every suggestion or experience he comes up with – but they never criticize or judge.

The Tip: Being comfortable with your desire means you'll know when you don't want to do something because it's outside your (hopefully widening) comfort zone or because it makes you feel downright uncomfortable. So you might not want to go skinny-dipping in the gym after hours (indecent loitering, anyone?), but you may go to a strip club on a whim (and even tip for a private lap dance).

The Trick: Casual sex is your bad-girl right:

❋ **If you're in a relationship**, "casual" might mean having a quickie when one of you is in the mood and the other isn't. Not every naked moment between you needs to be meaningful – bad girls know that sex can just be sex. *Vanilla*

❋ **If you're footloose and fancy free**, "casual" might mean having a guilt-free, no expectations one night stand. There are certain moments that rev up a girl's libido and she's just gotta have it: weddings, vacations, holiday parties, dance clubs, a bad day, a balmy night... you get the picture. These sort of encounters take a little finesse – never do them with a co-worker or your boss. Nip any expectations on his part in the bud by telling him you're not looking for a boyfriend: you just wanna have fun. Do this before the pants come off. Go to his place (it will be easier to leave – but just in case, make sure you have your phone, a friend knows where you are and you're a black belt). Always use a condom. Stick with standard stuff (plenty of enthusiastic squeezing, licking, sucking, stroking, rubbing, moaning and maybe even a little pinching) and when it's over, make a grand exit, telling him you had a great time. *Baaaadd*

Bad Girl Dare 5: Be Unbridled

Bad girls make time for sex. They can make whoopee all night, collapse in a satisfied stupor and still be ready for more fun the next morning. Getting it on isn't something on their To Do list; it's on their *Want* To Do Now list. They know how to let go of whatever else is going on in their lives and enjoy the moment, right now.

The Tip: Don't wait until you're in the mood. Arousal isn't like the measles, a condition you catch. It's a state of mind and body that you make happen. When you're in a deep clinch, just let your mind go. Don't worry about paying the bills, doing your laundry, catching up on your email. He'll love your bad-girl attitude of being so in deep in your dirty deed deux that nothing else matters.

The Trick: Don't ho-hum waiting for him – just pounce:

✳ Set the alarm for an early morning wake-up booty call. *Naughty*

❋ Send him to work hard and happy – instead of the usual quick peck, lock lips for a tongue-smashing, teeth-gnashing smooch. Give his front region a loving hug with your hands at the same time. As he responds – in about a minute – break off and send him on his way. He'll be counting the hours until he can come... home. *Baaaadd*

❋ At a party, drag him off to the bathroom for your own festivities. Remember to take your panties off before you leave the house. *Baaaadd*

❋ The next time he's settled on the couch to catch up on football or soccer, go on the offence and wriggle onto his lap, blocking his view. Slowly take off your top, working your cheeks into his tent pole at the same time. He'll be too busy making his own score to care how his team did. *Vanilla*

Bad Girl Dare 6: Be Uninhibited

Hey, bad girls scream, grunt and moan. They don't care how much noise they make, how long they take, if their belly is sticking out, their hair is a mess, their vagina is squirting or they let out a few toots. Sex is messy – especially if you do it right.

The Tip: Let loose, get sweaty and don't worry about what the outcome is or if your body looks weird in this position or what's going on with him (he's a big boy and he can take care of himself – see Bad Girl Dare: Be Unchivalrous, page 80).

The Trick: Lose your self-consciousness:

❋ Leave the
lights on.
Naughty

❋ Show your
pleasure – in
the middle of
intercourse, dig your
nails into his butt and
pull him in close. *Naughty*

❋ Relax those muscles – women
tend to get uptight about
climaxing and squeeze
their vagina as the big
moment approaches. If you can keep it loosy-
goosey, you'll experience an intense wave of
wa-hoo. *Naughty*

❋ Look him in the eye as you come. *Vanilla*

20 Wicked Ways Bad Girls Make Him Whimper

1 Bad girls tease. Straddle him and dangle your breasts over his face. Now pull away when he tries to kiss them. *Vanilla*

3 Bad girls wait for no man. Just come when you're ready. *Baaaadd*

2 Bad girls use his wand like a sex toy – grab it and put it exactly where you want it, when you need it most to bring yourself to orgasm. *Naughty*

4 Bad girls get straight to the point so skip the kisses and go down on him first thing. *Naughty*

5 Bad girls know how to tap into his fantasies. Mix up your kisses – make them soft, then hard, suck, then nibble. He'll feel like he's being seduced by a dozen women at once. *Vanilla*

6 Bad girls know he's not just a big dick – pay attention to his other body parts: Caress and stroke his back and neck and legs during sex to let him know you want *all* of him. *Vanilla*

7 A bad girl isn't afraid to tell him, touch by touch, what she's going to do to him, getting as graphic as she dares. *Baaaadd*

8 Bad girls touch themselves – not just down there, up there too. Get some lotion and rub it on your breasts during sex. *Baaaadd*

9 Bad girls put their whole sexy self into their BJs. Suck just the tip of his penis while squeezing the base of the shaft with your hands stacked on top each other. *Naughty*

10

Bad girls play rough – and he loves it. He's built tough, so stroke as hard as you dare, squeezing out his grand finale. *Baaaadd*

11

Bad girls don't let him get away with just the one orgasm. Have some cream handy designed to revive a drooping member by stirring up a slight burning sensation, improving blood flow and boosting his bad boy. *Baaaadd*

12. Bad girls know how to throw in an unexpected squeeze, pinch, tug or nibble. Playing rough sends an instant message to his brain that you're a wild wench and he is your he-man. *Baaaadd*

13 Bad girls know how to pump him up. Wrap your index finger and thumb around the base of his penis and without touching the rest of his shaft, alternately squeeze, creating a harder, more intense erection. *Vanilla*

Bad girls don't wait for the right moment to seduce his boys. Strike when an opportune moment arises – or make it happen. Unzip him when he's trying to talk on the phone (preferably to his mother or boss), while he's driving (give it two minutes before demanding that he pulls over so you can finish off the job properly) or just after he has emerged fresh and fragrant from the shower. *Baaaadd*

14

15

Bad girls know where his G-spot is. Technically called the prostate gland, you can find it by popping a well-lubed finger up his bottom, then curling it slightly and tap, tap, tapping against the wall of his rectum. *Baaaadd*

16 Bad girls never ignore the boys. Take each of his balls gently in your mouth and suck. *Naughty*

17 Bad girls know that more than deep-throating, what he really wants during oral sex is to watch you gobble him up. Have him stand facing the edge of the bed while you lie back flat on the mattress and open wide. *Naughty*

18 Bad girls know where his secret orgasm switch is – and how to flick it. Mid-way between the base of his penis and his butt is a smooth patch of flesh known as the perineum. Using strong pressure, massage it in a clockwise motion while squeezing hard on his shaft. Hold on tight! *Naughty*

19

Bad girls know how to draw out his pleasure until he begs for mercy. Squeeze the base of his penis as he's about to come and continue to exert pressure for about five seconds afterward. *Naughty*

20

Bad girls know that the sexiest thing you can do to him is exclaim how big he is. *Vanilla*

Bad Girl Dare 7: Be Unchivalrous

Bad girls know how to take. Selfishness may not be desirable in a relationship, but between the sheets it's a must. Bad girls love sex so they understand their desires and how to satisfy them.

The Tip: Do whatever it takes to get what you need in bed. If that means holding him off until you are ready, sending him south of your border, using a vibrator, flipping him on his back so you're on top, go for it. Don't worry – he'll be just as excited, knowing your moves are tipping you over the edge.

The Trick: Bad girls know that sexual selfishness doesn't mean that they don't help take care of his needs too:

✳ Don't wait for him to tell you what feels good – give him a special ball tug-shaft twirl, nipple pinch, deep-throated suck or whatever your signature mattress move might be (every bad girl has at least one) and ask how he likes it. And don't worry if all you get is a grunt or groan – you've made him incapable of speech, you little minx! *Naughty*

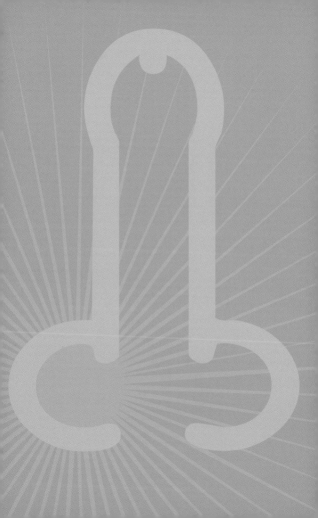

Bad Girl Dare 8: Be Unstoppable

Bad girls don't have bad sex. Ever. That's because if she accidentally ends up with a dud in the sack, she simply takes control of the situation. This means more than just getting on top (although that's always good) or tossing him around (and so is that). It's knowing and doing anything that makes *you* feel good – and making sure he knows and does it, too. So even if he still sucks, she still gets hers, but more likely, he gets into her in-control attitude and they both get theirs.

The Tip: One of the biggest complaints men make about mattress mambo is not having a clue what she needs. Bad girls don't just tell – they also show by taking charge of the sheet action.

The Trick: Good girls compromise. Bad girls have orgasms and do their best to make sure their partners do, too:

✳ Sit on his chest with your back to him and your bottom close to his chin. Focus on his genitals, bringing him to the brink of orgasm and then back again with your hands and mouth. Now rearrange your position slightly so your nipples and cleavage can become involved in the action, too. To stimulate yourself, rock between his collarbones (careful not to strangle him!) and then, when the time is right for you, wriggle forward and without turning around, let him enter you. *Naughty*

❋ Show him your love – for yourself, that is. Run your fingertips over your nipples and gently squeeze your breasts in your hands, all while holding eye contact with him. *Baaaadd*

❋ Be demanding. Say the words, "I want", "I need", "Put it in now", "Slow down", "Speed up". Sex is about the only time a guy will happily follow directions. *Naughty*

❋ Bad girls know where their G-spots are – now show him. Tell him to insert a finger in your vagina and stroke your G-spot with a come-hither motion during oral sex. *Naughty*

❋ As he goes down on you, wriggle your hips from side to side so his tongue hits every angle of your clitoris. *Vanilla*

✳ Help him out and play with yourself. Go slow so he can see just how it's done. *Baaaadd*

✳ Direct your orgasm – As you feel yourself reaching climax, slow down to an intensity of about 75 per cent of your full speed (in other words, you decide what the pace is – hold onto his hips and bring his penis out for air if he needs to reduce his throttle). Stay there for one minute and then pick up the pace again. This technique makes the end result even more intense. *Vanilla*

LUSTY LINGO

Untying her tongue may be one of the most difficult things for a good girl to do during sex. If you're not used to speaking up, it's hard to know what to say or how to say it without giggling. Try one of these bad-girl lines.

If you're not ready for F2F discourse, sext him what you want him to do. Time how fast he memorizes it! *Baaaadd*

Make an obscene phone call. Call him from another room and tell him he should meet you in the bedroom in five minutes. Be prepared to describe (whatever you are lusting for) in explicit detail (but triple-check the number before you press the send key.) *Baaaadd*

As you body jam, describe exactly what you're doing to each other and what you'd like done ("kiss my breasts", "touch me here – no, *here*"). *Baaaadd*

It's up to you how explicit you get – sometimes a saucy synonym says more than the most carnal curse word: "pound", "thrust", "drive", "stuff" and "cram" are all sexy stand-ins. *Naughty*

And the simplest vixeny vocalization? A happy groan that lets him know you are into whatever it is that he's doing. *Vanilla*

Bad girls know that the three sexiest phrases in the English language are: "I want you", "I'm coming" and " *Yes!*" *Vanilla*

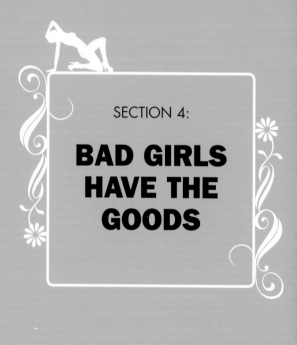

SECTION 4:

BAD GIRLS HAVE THE GOODS

Every bad girl has a bag of tricks that she carries in her purse in the same way that other women pack a tube of lipstick. These props are carefully selected to enhance her sexual experience – whether she's with a partner or alone. That's because bold babes know that sometimes a girl's gotta do what a girl's gotta do, so she might as well do it with full satisfaction. This willingness to be responsible for her own pleasure at all times and create her own opportunities is the very essence of what makes a bad girl good in bed.

Luckily, cheeky chicas are willing to spread the joy and share their toys. This is actually a good test of whether he's man enough to be with you. Gutsy guys know that bringing a vibrating penis or extra lube to bed doesn't mean he's a dud.

What Your Average-Dare She-Devil Packs These Days

❋ A bad girl never met a pair of Velcro cuffs she didn't like. Easy to compress and ultra-handy for impromptu tantalizing torture sessions. *Naughty*

❋ A vibrating cock ring guarantees you're in for hours of fun, whatever his personal best staying power. *Naughty*

❋ A beaded necklace (one without exposed string or wire) can be worn, then lubed up and wrapped around his penis for a fancy handjob. *Baaaadd*

❋ A small bullet vibrator can be slipped into your sex play, but it's much naughtier to give him a private demo of how you make yourself swoon. Or opt for a vibe that can be inserted during sex to give your booty shake an electric buzz. *Naughty*

❋ A Smartphone for taking off-the-cuff and off-with-the-clothes naughty snaps and videos. Just make sure you use yours so he doesn't get his own bad-boy ideas and post your buff in-the-buffs over the internet. Add an app for accessing a dirty movie (yes, porn – it's where bad girls get their most ribald ideas), turn on the vibrating ring and you have practically everything you need for a wanton rendezvous. *Naughty*

❋ Stash a tube of flavoured or heating lube to keep things juicy. *Vanilla*

❋ A scarf or stockings can pull multi-duty as a fashion accessory, a blindfold, wrist and ankle ties or an impromptu cock ring. Just practise your Scout knots or plan on carrying a pair of scissors as well. *Vanilla*

❋ A pocket mirror strategically placed parallel to his body will give him an eye-popping view as you bob for his apples. *Naughty*

Bad Girls' Checklist

Think of these as your essential list to total bad girl-dom.

You've Tried or Had:

- Anal sex *Baaaadd*

- S&M complete with tie up and smack down *Baaaadd*

- Pole dancing *Baaaadd*

- A threesome (you chose the gender combo) *Baaaadd*

- Snogging someone whose name you don't know *Baaaadd*

- Spending the day naked *Naughty*

- Sending a sext message *Vanilla*

- Taking nude photos of your boyfriend *Naughty*

- Making a triple-X video *Baaaadd*

- Getting it on at work *Baaaadd*

- Going on a date without underwear *Vanilla*

- Having sex that woke the neighbours *Baaaadd*

- Throwing a drink in your boyfriend's face *Vanilla*

- Flirting with his friends *Vanilla*

- Going topless at the beach *Naughty*

- A lap dance (on the receiving or giving end) *Naughty*

- A one-night stand *Baaaadd*

- Sex with a toyboy and/or sugar daddy *Baaaadd*

- Making love all night and into the next morning *Vanilla*

- Multiple orgasms *Vanilla*

You Own (and Use):

- At least one porn movie – which is watched regularly for both pleasure and inspiration *Naughty*

- At least one vibrator *Naughty*

- A dirty mouth *Naughty*

- Crotchless panties *Naughty*

- A tattoo *Naughty*

- A booty-call friend *Baaaadd*

- A piercing below the neck *Baaaadd*

Seven Really Bad Moves
Bad Girls *Never* Do

1
Anything that puts their life at risk

2
Fake it

3
Skimp on safe sex

4
Skip birth control when a baby isn't on the agenda

5
Get arrested

6
Stay with a man who isn't her type

7
Waste time on a guy who isn't interested

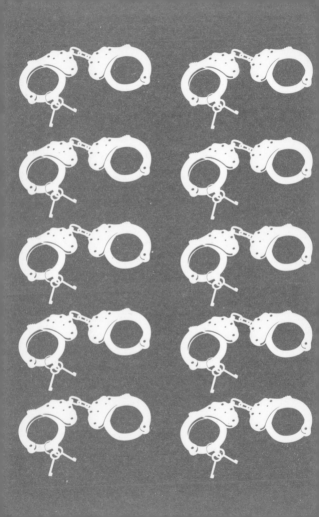